Connecting Up

By
Mary Ellen Hopkins

For William Matthew Hopkins
born January 15, 1990,
with love from Grandma Hopkins

Quilt in progress!

On back of quilt.

Table of Contents

Ready for a new way of piecing those little right triangles?

Want to keep all those little points nice and sharp?

Want to find out what sharing the corner means?

Check this out..............

Connector Blocks separate main design blocks, open up a design, and "connect" the design blocks together. The open space created by these blocks may be used for accentuating the overall design, and they provide space for "drop feed dog" quilting. The main design block may be any size and may be a combination of smaller design blocks.

In the following pages of this section you will see several examples of connector blocks, including different applications of the connector block construction technique. You will see the general technique of constructing connectors and each design shows a breakdown of blocks. Where a special construction technique is necessary, it is presented.

I have chosen not to present the construction instructions for the design blocks in this book. You will find excellent descriptions of these in my "The It's Okay If You Sit On My Quilt Book" and "Baker's Dozen Doubled" books. Those of you familiar with my techniques through classes should note that the Connector Block construction in this book does not involve Perfect Pieced Traingles. This is a foot stomper!

On to the good stuff. Have fun!

Connectors from "It's Okay..." book
pages 110-111

I have always wanted to expand on the work begun in the "It's Okay..." book using Connectors. So let's begin with the blocks on pages 110 and 111.

In this first example on the left, I have taken the Split 9-Patch on page 110 and expanded it 9 times.

But look how much more interesting the design becomes when you add a Connector Block the same size as 4 little Split 9-Patches. instead! The design has so much more potential and personality now!

It is also open to many possibilities for machine quilting.

And here is the Grand Finale from page 111!
It has Connectors, is on the diagonal, and has been expanded!

The possibilities seem endless when using Conncector Blocks as you willl see throughout this book.

Turn the page and begin to experience a new way of piecing triangles!

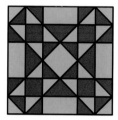 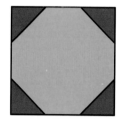

Pieced blocks, joined together with a Connector Block.

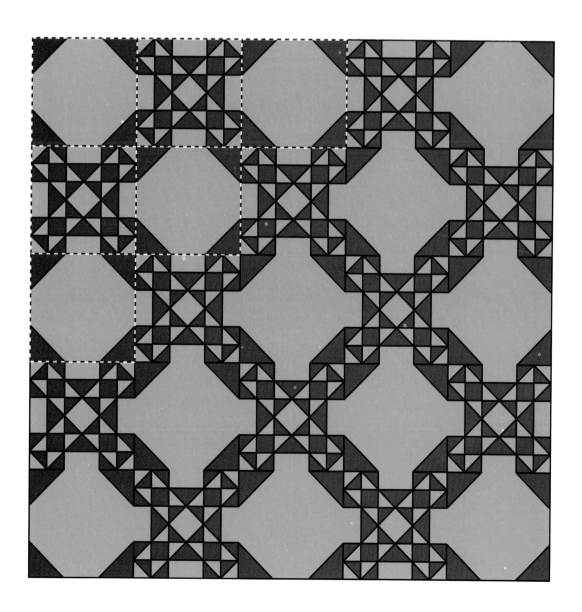

Connector Blocks —

When you have completed your design blocks
turn one over and measure raw edge to raw edge
of the square you want your connector corner
to line up with.

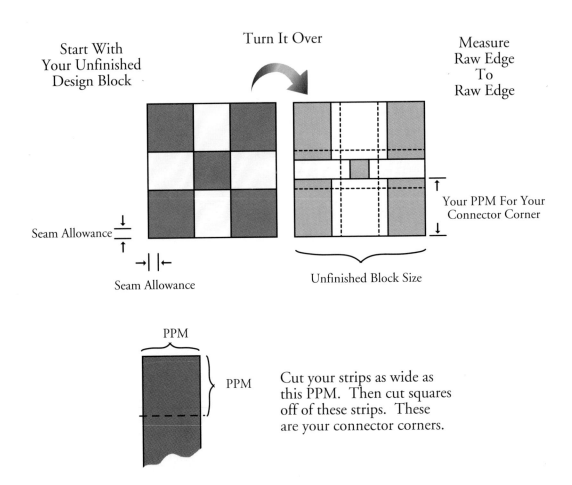

Start With
Your Unfinished
Design Block

Turn It Over

Measure
Raw Edge
To
Raw Edge

Seam Allowance

Seam Allowance

Your PPM For Your
Connector Corner

Unfinished Block Size

PPM

PPM

Cut your strips as wide as
this PPM. Then cut squares
off of these strips. These
are your connector corners.

Place connector corners on each corner of blocks
made of the background fabric of your choice.
These blocks will be made to the same measurement as your design block raw edge to raw edge.

Place the connector corners against the background blocks right sides together as shown.

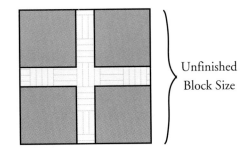

Unfinished
Block Size

— Not Just Another Pretty Corner

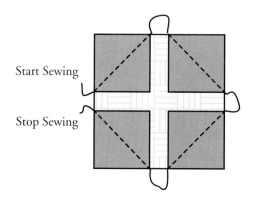

Start Sewing

Stop Sewing

Sew across the diagonals of each connector square. It is easy and probably most efficient to sew all of the corners on one connector block without cutting the thread (as shown.)

Trim off the outside corners of each connector corner. This cleans up the corner of your connector block.

*Do not cut off the corner of your background block! This is needed to ensure the final connector block is square and the same size as the design block! ***

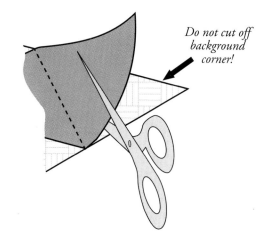

Do not cut off background corner!

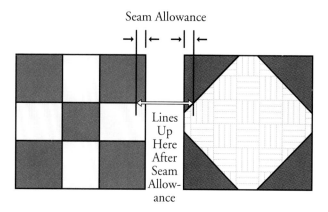

Trimmed Edge

Seam

Now fold the corner squares back over the seam and press. The corners may not quite match up with the background corner. That is why you use the background to line up when combining blocks!

Your design and connector blocks are now the same size. Sew these together as usual.

Note that the connector corners appear larger than the corner squares of your design block. Remember, they are the same size raw edge to raw edge. Your seam allowance will line them up.

Seam Allowance

Lines Up Here After Seam Allow-ance

*** Editor's Note: Mary Ellen is thought to have a hit squad roving the country and willing to break the kneecaps of anyone attempting to cut off these corners.*

Shadings...

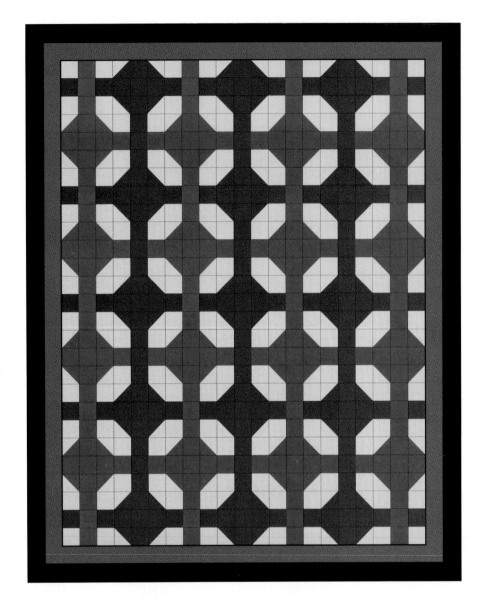

I have always wanted to expand Page 25 in my It's Okay book. The next few pages will give you a good start on exploring the many possibilities for this page.

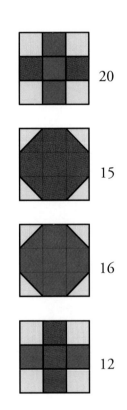

20

15

16

12

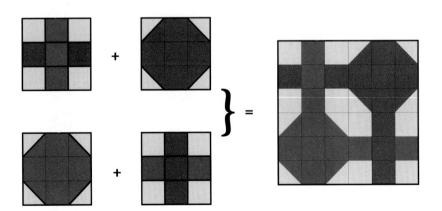

... of Page 25

Playing with the pieced block is almost as much
fun as putting it all together! Page 25 of the
"It's Okay..." book is about one of the most versatile
blocks that you can manipulate.

On these two pages I have shown you only a few
of the many ways you can shade this block and get
many interesting overall designs.

On the previous page you get a look similar to
'Round the Twist, and on this page you get a
chain link look by shading in a horizontal
direction.

The photograph at the bottom right shows a
two color plus background shading for a
very graphic effect.

These two pages give many possibilities for showing
the versatility of the simple pieced block.

Make sure you take a night - or five - out of your life
to play with page 14.

Page 25 Interpretation
By Mary Ellen Hopkins

Metamorphosis

This quilt can be very easy when you realize that it is nothing more than two different 3–Patches in each row. I have shown the breakdown for some of the rows here. You will easily recognize the remaining blocks. This one could go on and on and…

Metamorphosis
Designed, Pieced, and Quilted
By Mary Ellen Hopkins

Worksheet #1
for page 25 in "It's Okay ..." book

Worksheet # 2

for page 25 in "It's Okay..." book

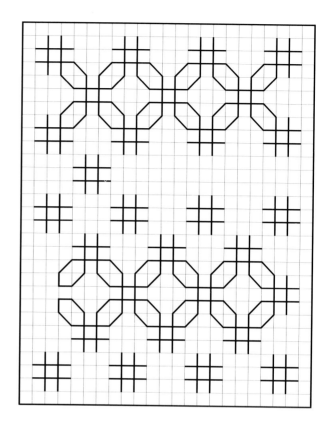

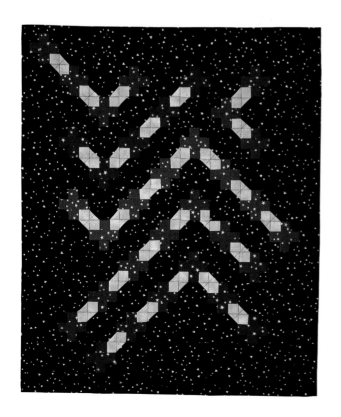

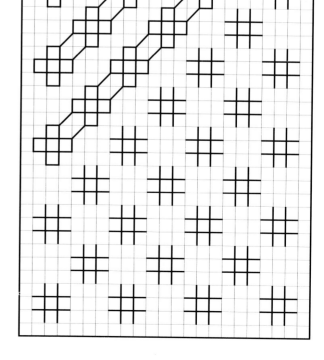

Star Quilt By Mary Ellen Hopkins

The Amazing Bowtie

Struggling to make your Bowties?

See…

rip defying feats
of fabrication

See…

the big bowtie building
bonanza!

See…

how these blocks seemingly
fall into place!

When you use Connector Blocks it's
as snappy as a clip–on!

And now it's time to tie one on…

The Amazing Bowtie Construction Technique

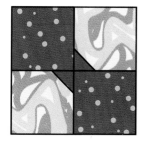

These little bow-ties truly are amazing. One of the amazing things is how easy they are to make. With this technique, these little blocks just "pop" out like popcorn! To make this block, just follow the simple steps shown here.

Cut an equal, even number of squares of the two colors above. Sample sizes are shown on page 22.) Cut the same number of connector corner squares. lay the connector corners on the background squares right sides together.

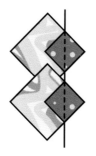

String through.

Trim the corners as shown on page 9.

Press back over the seam.

String through and cut into pairs.

Lay out the squares as shown and flip over right sides together as indicated by arrows.

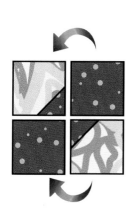

Finger Press Up

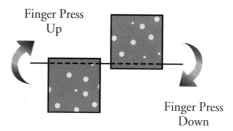

Finger Press Down

Lay them out as shown below and finger press open in direction of arrows. This is how the pieces should look to you as you stand over them before you finger press them open.

Open up and flip over right sides together as indicated by arrow.

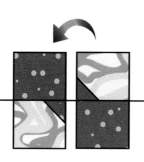

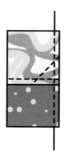

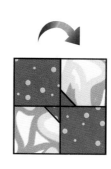

String through.

Press Open. Voila!

Putting The Amazing Bowtie Together

Very easy - but thought provoking (you'll need a 3-minute egg timer.)

One strip of each will yield 8 Bowties

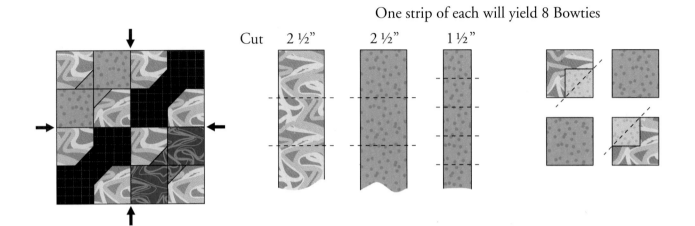

A unit of 4 will be approximately 7 - 8". Make lots of these units. 48 units would be about 45" by 60". You'll need ¾ yards each of light aqua and dark aqua, 1 yard of rust, and 2 yards of background.

Now it's time for the 3-minute egg timer, 'cause you have a decision to make. You can make

1) Straight Furrows,

2) Barn Raising (Page 21, "It's Okay…"), or

3) 9-Patch Setup (page 47, "It's Okay…")

1) Straight Furrows   2) Barn Raising   3) 9-Patch Setup

Amazing Bowtie Layouts

Let's look at some layouts with different sized bowties. Here is how to make blocks for these layouts:

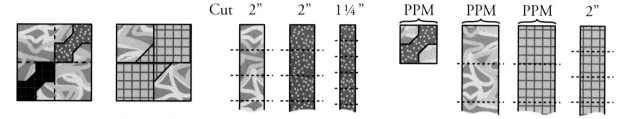

Cut 2"   2"   1 ¼"   PPM   PPM   PPM   2"

Make the small Bowtie first and measure raw edge to raw edge for your PPM for the larger Bowtie squares.

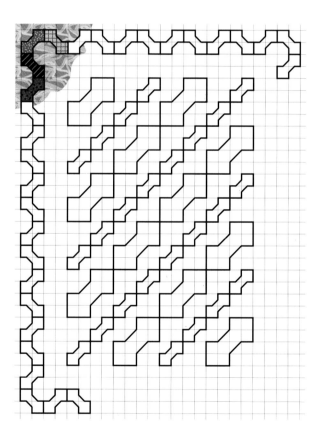

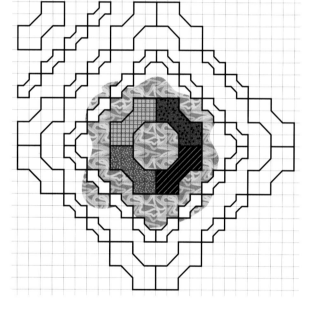

There are some very interesting ways to put these Bowties together. Note the barnraising set above. Now tilt the page. It goes on and on and…

The above layout is about 40" x 52" (using the above construction sizes), including the terrrific border. It takes
- 12 big Bowties,
- 24 little ones, and
- 52 little ones in the border.

Although this is a 2 bell block, it is still very simple and plain in shape. Therefore, I think it really needs a busy background fabric. For even greater effect, try two background fabrics.

Bowties, By Mary Ellen Hopkins

Bowtie Quilt
Mary Ellen Hopkins

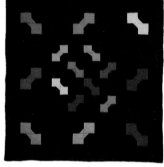

Which Way Is UP?
By Joanna Myrick
Templeton, CA

Bowtie Quilt
By Barbara Kaempfer
Mettmenstetten, Switzerland

Buttons & Bows
By Cindy McDonald
Iowa Falls, IA

First Quilt For William
By Mary Ellen Hopkins

In this first quilt for
my first grandson,
William, I used an offset
Barn Raising set and
added an initial for
his last name. See
page 62 for a closeup.
This is one of my
best fabric pulls.

. . . and that's the size of it!

Squares:	cut 2"
Corners:	cut 1 ¼ "
Finished Block:	approx. 3"

Your expectations of finished
sizes might be different from
the actual finished product,
unless you plan ahead.
For instance, the finished sizes
of the Amazing Bow-Tie block
are dramatically different for
half-inch increments in the
width of strips cut for
the squares.

Squares:	cut 2½ "
Corners:	cut 1½ "
Finished Block:	approx. 4"

Squares:	cut 3½ "
Corners:	cut 2"
Finished Block:	approx. 6"

Squares:	cut 3"
Corners:	cut 1 ¾ "
Finished Block:	approx. 5"

The sizes indicated here
are the <u>cutting</u> sizes for
the squares and corners.

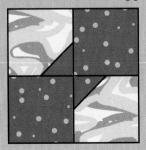

"CALM, THOUGHTFUL ORGANIZATION IS THE KEY" *

Editor's Note: If you don't think this is a quote from Mary Ellen, just ask her!

Let The St★rs Get In Your Eyes!

Stars have these little pointy things sticking out which cry out for connector construction techniques. (Actually, they don't really cry out. They sort of whine in an annoying way.)

Stars should twinkle.

It is perfectly possible to have different sized stars in the same quilt.

Miniature stars can be solid.

Stars larger than 2" square should be made of larger prints

Since the four patch star is a relatively uncomplicated shape, I think the background ought to have a lot of movement.

Larger stars need larger prints.

Perhaps we'll become quilting stars while quilting stars. So let's get started!

Tip For Starrier Stars

The measurements given for these stars are set up so that the base of the points of the stars meet exactly at the center square of the star.

You should add a smidgin (has anyone ever measured a smidgin?) to the corner squares' dimension to ensure that the points are not separated when they are attached to the star center square. This allows for error and makes for starrier stars.

Extra overlap gives room for error.

Not enough overlap creates gaps when pieces are sewn together.

Overlap is acceptable.

Size in the quilt (after seam allowances)

There is a gap between points.

Connecting Up the 4-Patch Star

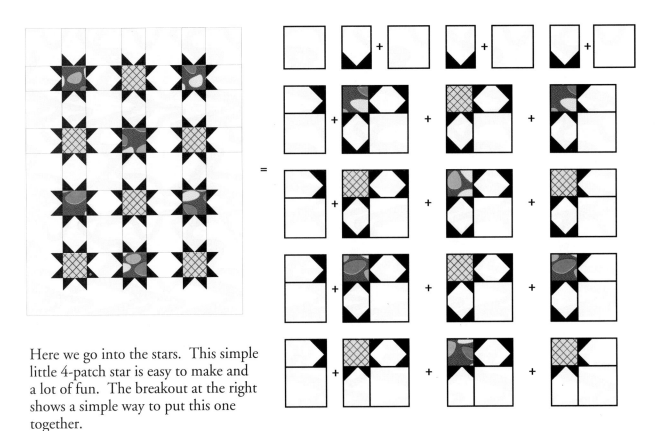

Here we go into the stars. This simple little 4-patch star is easy to make and a lot of fun. The breakout at the right shows a simple way to put this one together.

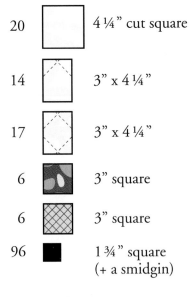

20		4 ¼" cut square
14		3" x 4 ¼"
17		3" x 4 ¼"
6		3" square
6		3" square
96		1 ¾" square (+ a smidgin)

4-Patch Star By Mary Ellen Hopkins

24

Stars On The Diagonal

The 4-patch star looks wonderful on the diagonal as well, doesn't it? This one requires floating with large and small triangles, as well as corner triangles. Stars on the diagonal can be quilted in rows. This one can be pieced with different colored star points, or all the same color. These diagonal 4-patch stars, take borders beautifully.

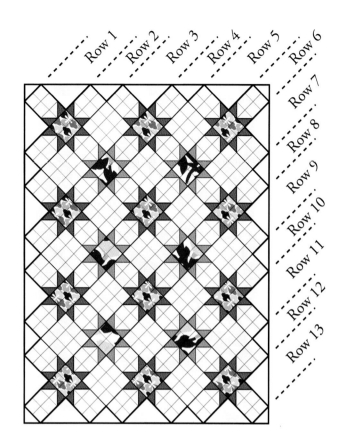

If all star points are the same color use the following pieces:

17	⬜	4 ¼" square
24	🔺	3" x 4 ¼"
24	🔷	3" x 4 ¼"
12	▦	3" square
6	▨	3" square
48	▪	1 ¾" square
96	▪	(+ a smidgin)

24	🔷	
144	▪	
24	🔺	

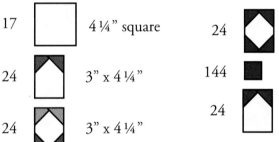

4	◻	9" square for large triangles for floating
3	◻	7" square for small triangles for floating
2	◻	4 ¼" square for corners

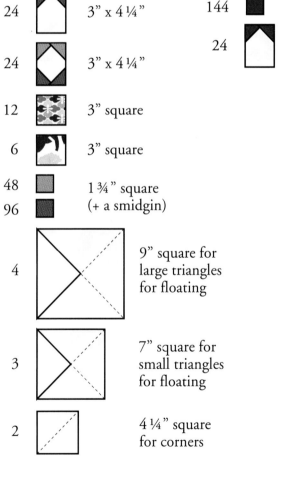

Diagonal 4-Patch Star
By Mary Ellen Hopkins

25

Here is another variation on the diagonal 4-Patch Star. Note the busy background fabric livens up the simpler star shape. The 3-Patch stars in the border are described on page 41. The H is on page 51.

The Star, The Windowpaning, and The Pieced Block

There are several things you need to consider before you decide on the size of your stars and your windowpanes. If the basic requirement is to highlight the pieced block, you want to be care—ful not to overpower it with your stars.

With this in mind, here are two simple rules to follow:

If there is a high contrast between the star and the windowpaning (for example, the star is significantly darker than the windowpaning), the star and windowpaning should be smaller.

The darker the star, the smaller it should be. Conversely, lighter stars may be larger (if the contrast is not too great.)

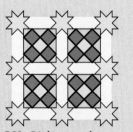

OK. Light stars, low contrast do not overpower the pieced block.

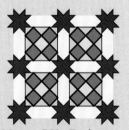

Not so OK. Dark stars, high contrast tend to interfere with the pieced block.

OK. Dark stars, high contrast are countered with smaller stars, narrower windowpaning.

OK. The effect of darker stars is reduced with less windowpaning contrast.

The illustrations here demonstrate these rules. The pieced blocks here are all the same size.

Stars And Churn Dash Blocks

Pieced Block Orientation

How you put your star quilt together may depend on the type of pieced block or large pattern block you use. For example, the Churn Dash is a block that really should be on the diagonal.

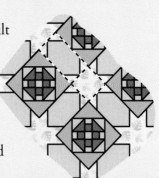

4-Patch Stars and Churn Dash
By Kathryn Small
Westwood, CA

3-Patch Stars and Churn Dash
By Kathryn Small
Westwood, CA

An Alternate Star Layout

A 4 pointed star can be substituted for the eight 4-Patch star. The layout is roughly the same. The windowpaning pieces have only one connector at each end as indicated. You might try combining 4-Patch and 4 pointed stars.

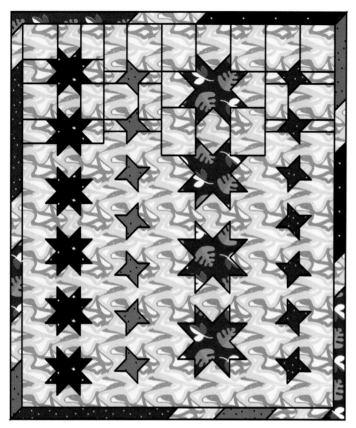

Strings of Stars

Here is a neat way to combine several different sized blocks in a STARtling quilt. By putting each type of block in a single strip as shown below, you can then combine strips. And there are no blocks to line up when combining strips!

Once your strips are made you can arrange them in the most pleasing order. If you have a lot of background fabric, you could make long strips, one at a time over a long period of time.

Note: Small stars, small prints
Medium stars, medium prints
Large stars, large prints

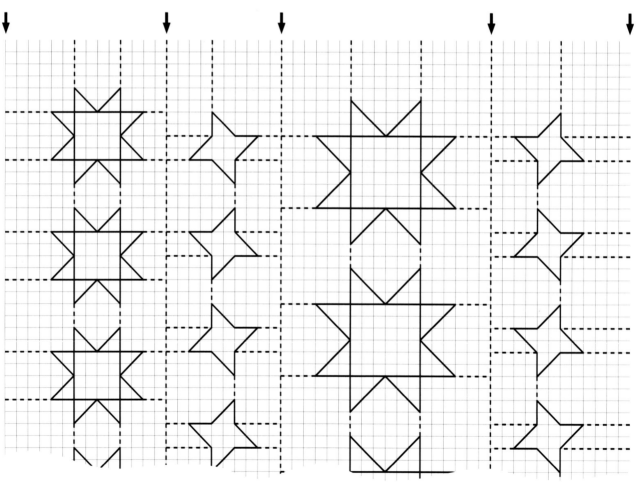

Strings of Stars By Mary Ellen Hopkins

Stars Over The Lobster Shack
Two Lights, Maine

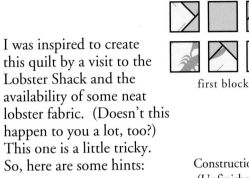

PPM {

first block

second block

I was inspired to create this quilt by a visit to the Lobster Shack and the availability of some neat lobster fabric. (Doesn't this happen to you a lot, too?) This one is a little tricky. So, here are some hints:

The small stars are the starting point. Piece them first. The center of the star is the basic PPM for this quilt. (Look at the grid here, choose your proportional finished sizes of the pieces, then add twice your seam allowance in each dimension.)

You will make three basic blocks for this quilt. The interior of the large star is a simple 3-patch (first basic block), which gives the length for the short side of the rectangular block (second basic block).

For the third basic block, the first basic block is expanded. The corner pieces are half again as large as the center of the small star (finished size). The pieces with the points are lengthened to this same finished size. The unfinished block width gives the length of the second basic block, to which the large star points are attached.

Construction (Unfinished Sizes)

PPM {

third block

Since this quilt is on the diagonal, it should be pieced in strips. (The row of stars at the bottom is also pieced in a strip, however it is on the straight and attached last.) You will also need triangles for floating.

Stars Over The Lbster Shack

Stars Over The Lobster Shack
By
Mary Ellen Hopkins
(I think it's
a 4-Star Restaurant)

Stars Over The Lobster Shack
Variation By
Mary Beth Seeley
West Los Angeles, CA

CIRCLE of STARS

Okay, everybody.
It's graph paper time!
Here is a design I
worked out in
July of 1988 and
it looks wonderful.
But, it's not for the
faint of heart.

You have to be very careful to get the sizes right here. First, carefully look at the grid and see what pieces you will cut, and note the relative sizes in the finished quilt. You will need to decide what your unit of measurement will be. For example, you might choose one inch per grid square. Next you must add two of your seam allowances in each direction. For example, if a finished piece will be 2" x 3" and you have a ¼" seam allowance, you must cut the piece 2 ½" by 3 ½".

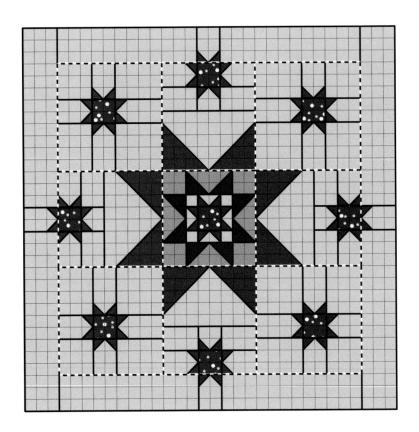

It is important that you don't make a block at a time. Instead, make all similar pieces at the same time (as indicated in the figure.)
Note that the solid lines on the figure denote the pieces within each block.
First, piece the center of the large star. Start with the small star and work your way out. Note that you will develop PPMs as you go.
Next piece the four corner blocks, the middle side blocks, and finally the strips (top and bottom first, then the sides.) Finally, sew the blocks together. Now you're ready for borders. Isn't this exciting?

Circle of Stars
By
Danita Rafalovich
Los Angeles, CA

Aren't the
backs
wonderful?

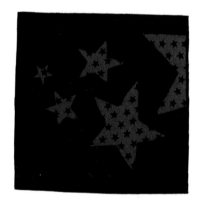

Circle of Stars
By
Danita Rafalovich
Los Angeles, CA

Stars & Hearts

(New Year's Eve, 1989, on which Mary Ellen was not invited to any parties)

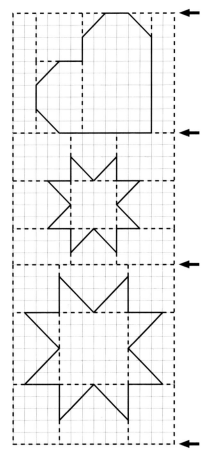

The design above represents finished sizes. Each grid square is ¾". The table below shows required cut sizes for finished sizes.

Table of Sizes

Grid Scale	Finished Size	Cut Size
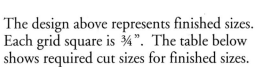	1½"	2"
	2¼"	2¾"
	3"	3½"
	3¾"	4¼"
	4½"	5"
	7½"	8"

Even though the separate blocks are different sizes (widths are the same, but height varies), the diagonal is true. To keep same length strips and a true diagonal, you should use a repeat of the three blocks. This one looks good as a 4 by 6.

It was necessary to come up with a design on this date because, while working in the shop that afternoon, I had become obsessed with four fabrics and I needed a home for them.

Two light greens, a light green with pink (the hearts), and my black with silver stars as a background were clamoring to be in the same quilt, so I obliged them. (They're seemingly content now, as you can see on the facing page.)

Since I only had the TV to hang out with, I was able to celebrate New Year's Eve four times while I sewed this one up.

Stars & Hearts
(New Year's Eve 1989)

Big and Little Stars

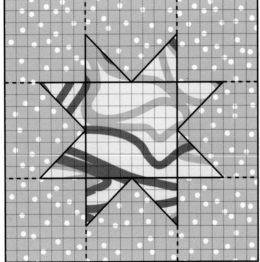

Approximately 8" square
(raw edge to raw edge)

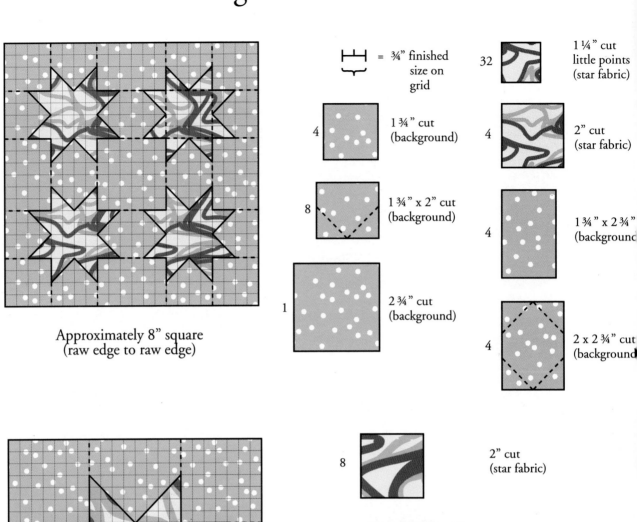

= ¾" finished size on grid

4 — 1 ¾" cut (background)

8 — 1 ¾" x 2" cut (background)

1 — 2 ¾" cut (background)

32 — 1 ¼" cut little points (star fabric)

4 — 2" cut (star fabric)

4 — 1 ¾" x 2 ¾" cut (background)

4 — 2 x 2 ¾" cut (background)

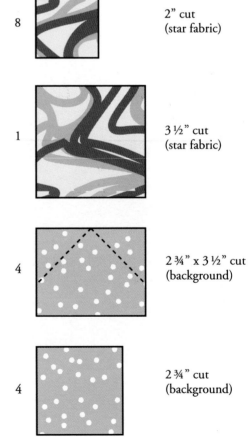

8 — 2" cut (star fabric)

1 — 3 ½" cut (star fabric)

4 — 2 ¾" x 3 ½" cut (background)

4 — 2 ¾" cut (background)

To see how these blocks fit into the quilt,
just turn your head to the right.

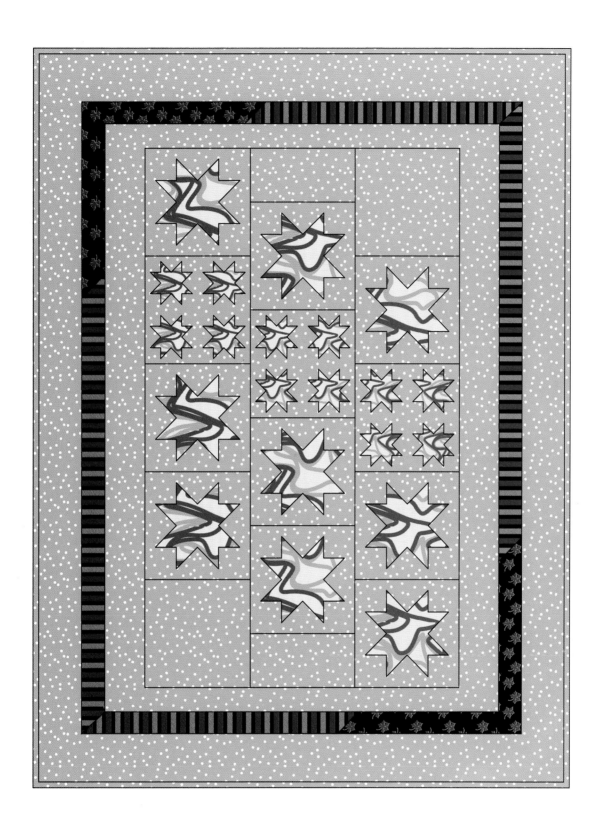

Combine the blocks on the facing page in strips and sew the strips together with the blocks offset by half a block. The results are wonderful and there are no seams to line up. You can easily add one or more borders to frame your favorite stars.

A Stellar Combination

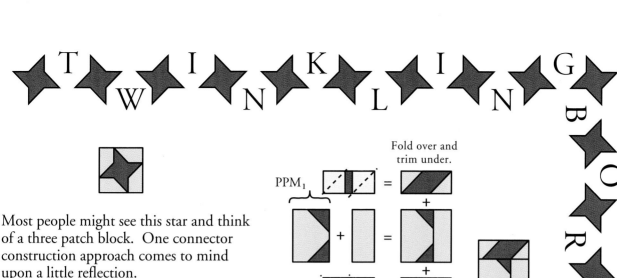

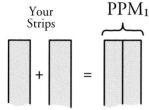

Most people might see this star and think of a three patch block. One connector construction approach comes to mind upon a little reflection.
However, don't do it this way................

Your Strips   PPM$_1$

Sew strips together, press, and measure raw edge to raw edge.

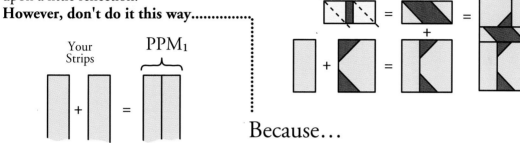

Fold over and trim under.

PPM$_1$

Because…

after more thought, you will see that with the above approach your points will be lost.

Now, if you just widen the block a little as shown below left this will never happen. This requires another PPM, but … no problem!
Now isn't this easy? And this will sparkle up many a quilt. See the quilt on page 28 as an example.

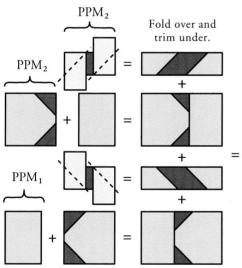

PPM$_2$

Fold over and trim under.

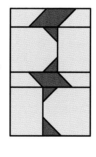

PPM$_1$ Your Strip   PPM$_2$

Sew strips together, press, and measure raw edge to raw edge.

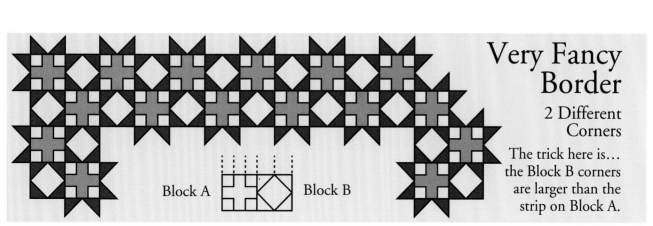

Very Fancy Border

2 Different Corners

The trick here is… the Block B corners are larger than the strip on Block A.

Block A   Block B

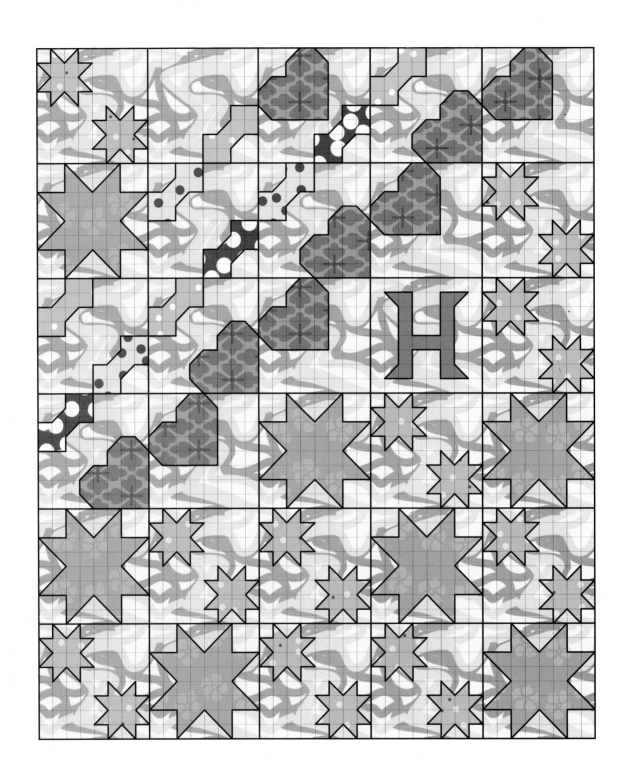

The Stars of the Show

(With a Hint of Things to Come)

You've Got To Have He♥rts!

Heart Quilt By Myrna Allen
Los Angeles, CA

This short section shows you how to make those neat little hearts and gives you a couple of layout options. These little hearts are a lot of fun and can mean a lot to someone special, even if it's you. I'm sure you will enjoy putting some of these together and perhaps giving someone you love a heartfelt gift. Now, doesn't the prospect of all of this make your heart beat a little faster? Let's get going and make one… from the heart

Heart Quilt By Harriet Berk
Santa Barbara, CA

Take heart!

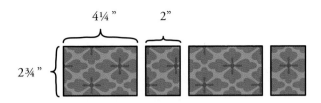

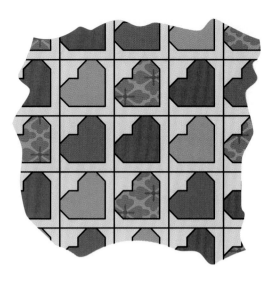

Cut strips of your selected heart fabric 2¾" wide and whomp off an equal numbers of 4¼" and 2" rectangles from these strips. Each 44" strip should yield six hearts.

You will also need to cut 1¼" strips of your background and cut these into 1¼" squares. Each strip should be enough for approximately eight hearts with some left over.

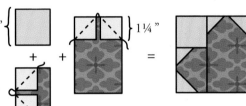

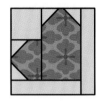

You can make the above heart quilt by adding some additional background material to two sides of the heart block (making sure to keep the block square.) This block was used in the quilts on the previous page.

You will need to cut 2" strips of your background fabric and cut off 2" squares for each heart. One strip will give you enough for approximately 20 hearts.

Use previously discussed connector construction techniques for the top and sides of the heart (right sides together, sew diagonal, trim underneath.) Then piece the rest together.

Heart To Heart

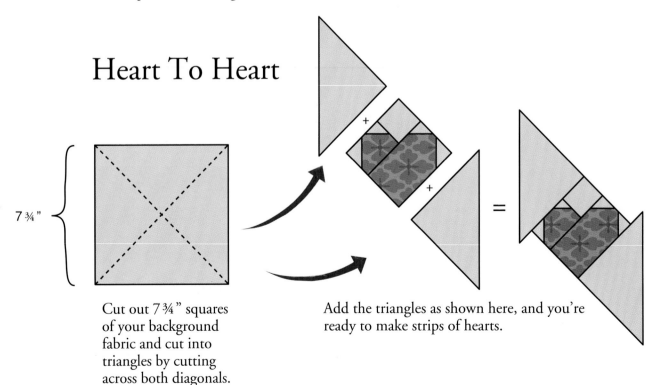

Cut out 7¾" squares of your background fabric and cut into triangles by cutting across both diagonals.

Add the triangles as shown here, and you're ready to make strips of hearts.

After you have constructed the sets of hearts and triangles, combine them as shown here. The points of the heart blocks must line up with each other.

Before sewing strips together, since the edges of your strips probably will be rough, trim all strips to the same width as the narrowest strip. To trim a strip, fold the bottom up to the top, line up selected points of heart blocks, and trim edges (as indicated on the right.) Sew strips together after lining up as shown below.

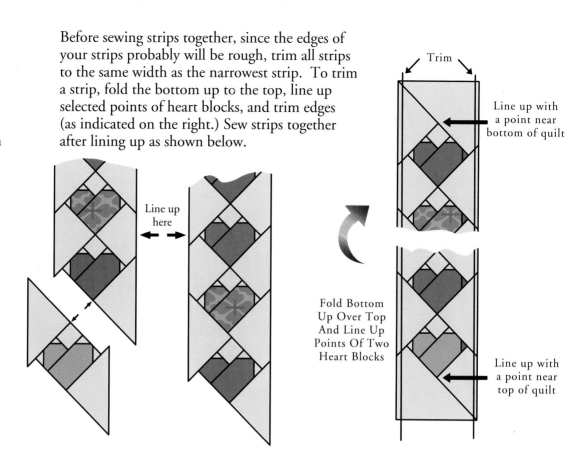

Line up here

Trim

Line up with a point near bottom of quilt

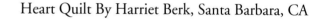

Fold Bottom Up Over Top And Line Up Points Of Two Heart Blocks

Line up with a point near top of quilt

Expensive Little Hearts By Mary Ellen Hopkins.

Heart Quilt By Harriet Berk, Santa Barbara, CA

'Round The Twist

A new way of constructing this popular design I developed in 1979, it is a repeat of 16 blocks for overall design. This technique for 'Round The Twist uses a connector block because I think it is much easier than other methods. Being easier also makes it more efficient!

To be effective, this design requires 5 fabrics:

> **2 strong (colors 1 and 2)**
> **2 medium (colors 3 and 4)**
> **1 background**

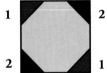

Block 1

Block 2

Block 3

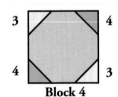

Block 4

Row 1   **Row 2**   **Row 3**

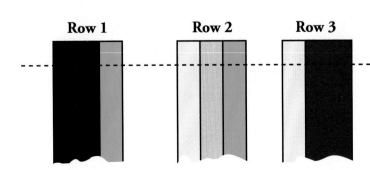

This is the cutting plan for Block 2. Follow directions for the connector block found on pages 8 and 9. Measure your PPM from 2 strips of row 2.

44

Round The Twist, By Barbara Spielberg, West Los Angeles, CA

Be careful on your finished grid size! I think 1" is too small. I like 1¼" best,
1½" not bad, but 1¾" is awfully big.

Grandmother's Cross

Grandmother's Cross is usually done in an 8-Patch using triangles, squares and rectangles. However, you can do it with a simple 3-Patch (you remember how to do that, don't you?) and can be finished using connector techniques as shown below.

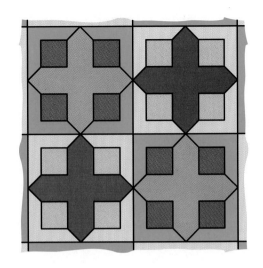

Start by making and attaching the top and bottom borders of the 3-patch and then make the sides based on the dimensions of this augmented 3-patch.

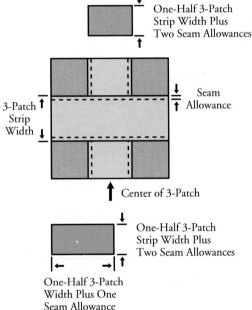

One-Half 3-Patch
Strip Width Plus
Two Seam Allowances

3-Patch
Strip
Width

Seam
Allowance

Center of 3-Patch

One-Half 3-Patch
Strip Width Plus
Two Seam Allowances

One-Half 3-Patch
Width Plus One
Seam Allowance

The points of the cross will be made from the same strips used for the cross in the 3-Patch. Whomp of rectangles with height equal to one-half the strip width plus two seam allowances.

The remainder of the top and bottom border requires pieces cut from strips with width equal to the height of the point pieces and length equal to one-half of the side of the 3-Patch plus one seam allowance.

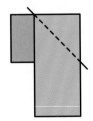

Place right sides together and sew across the diagonal (remember you can be off the diagonal in the direction of the corner but not in the other direction!)

Fold across the seam and trim the underside of the folded piece. (Another reminder: remember the hit squad.)

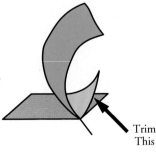

Trim
This

This should be the result.

Now complete the other side of the top (and bottom) borders of the patch in the same way. Place pieces right sides together and stitch across the diagonal.

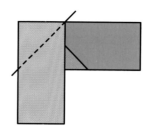

Fold over and trim the underside of the folded fabric.

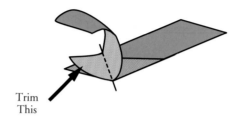

Trim This

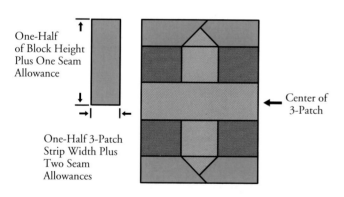

This should be the result.

Now attach the borders to the top and bottom of the 3-Patch block. The seam allowance will make the points of the cross match up with the center of the 3-Patch.

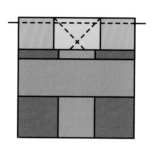

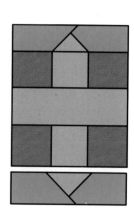

One-Half of Block Height Plus One Seam Allowance

One-Half 3-Patch Strip Width Plus Two Seam Allowances

← Center of 3-Patch

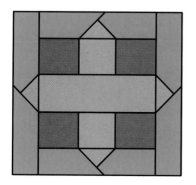

The rectangles for the points of the cross for the sides will be cut the same as for the top and bottom, using the same strips used for the cross in the 3-Patch.

The remainder of the side border requires pieces cut from strips with width equal to the height of the point rectangles and length equal to one-half of the side of the 3-Patch (with top and bottom borders sewn on) plus one seam allowance.

The construction of the side borders is exactly the same process as shown for the top and bottom borders.

The excess around the outside will disappear when the Grandmother's Cross blocks are sewn together. That is, the excess should be equal to one seam allowance, and points of adjacent blocks will touch.

Grandmother's Cross Alternate Layout

Grandmother's Cross can also be constructed in the layout shown here. This layout gives two looks to the design, with one set of crosses inside the other. The approach to this is different fabrics on the outside of the block.

Alternate Layout

Grandmother's Cross By Danita Rafalovich
Los Angeles, CA

Grandmother's Cross By Mary Beth Seeley
West Los Angeles, CA

Mary Ellen's Shoofly Pie

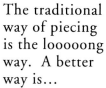

The traditional way of piecing is the looooong way. A better way is...

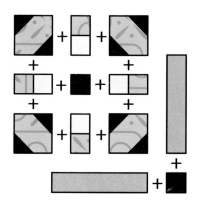

...the NEW way of piecing using Connectors.

Shoofly Quilt
By Marguerite Lu
Los Angeles, CA

Keeping A Lookout

The connector block and connector construction technique have potential for use on many blocks other than those already shown. I have found several that fit into this category, and I'm sure there are many others. Among the ones I have found are The H quilt (page 51 in "It's Okay"), the 3-Patch T (page 39 in "It's Okay"), Sailing Ship (page 42 in "It's Okay"), and Ribbon Bow (page 65 in "It's Okay"). Do things the easy way whenever you can. Keep a sharp lookout for connector applications. Now, let's look at these examples to help you recognize how connector construction applies.

H Quilt By Mary Ellen Hopkins

Give Someone Special A Little H

Do you know a Henry, Herbert, Harvey, Harold, or Hilbert who needs a quilt? Give him a little H and tell him to stop whining.

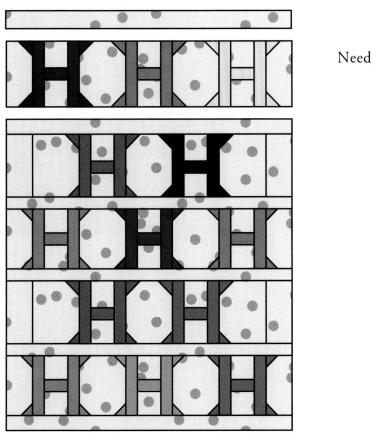

Your quilt should be approximately 24" x 31" at this stage

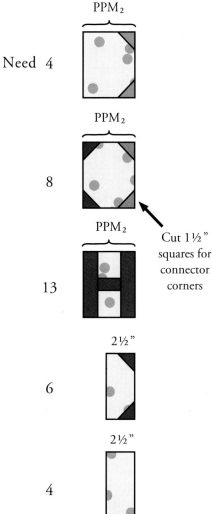

Need 4

8

13

6

4

Cut 1½" squares for connector corners

The height of all above blocks is PPM$_1$

For each "H" I strongly recommend a different fabric. For each you'll need 1½" strips approximately 20" long.

Step 1   Step 2

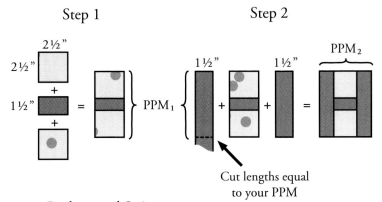

Cut lengths equal to your PPM

Background Strips:

1½" for strips between rows (and top and bottom)
2½" for side blocks and centers of H's
4½" for large background blocks (approximately, depending upon PPM$_2$)

1½ yds should be plenty (you can always use the extra for other stuff)

Terrific QuilTs (for Tim or Tom or Ted or Todd)

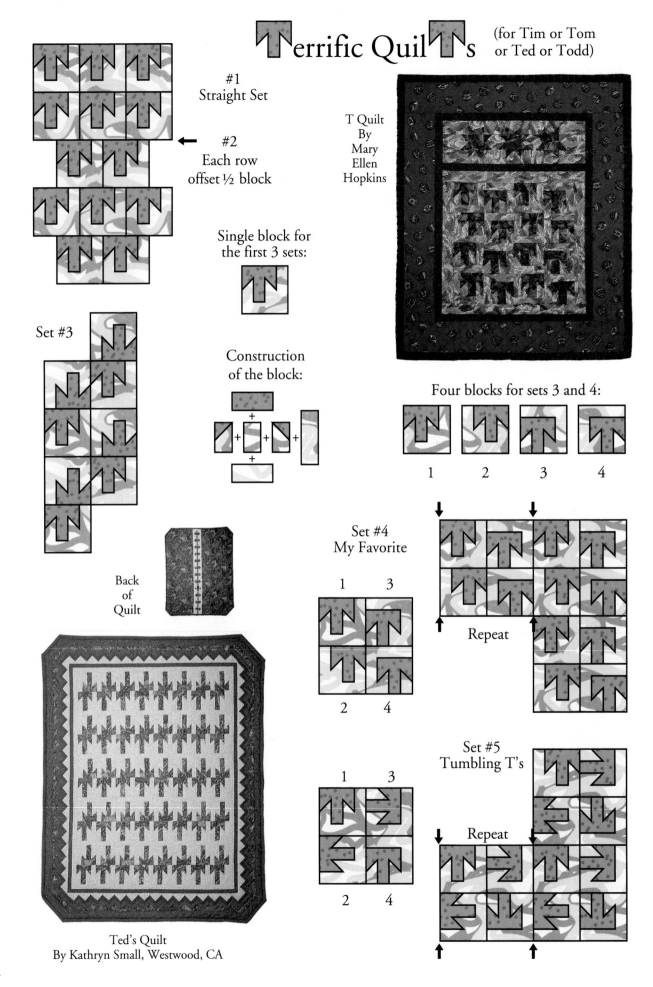

#1
Straight Set

#2
Each row
offset ½ block

Single block for
the first 3 sets:

Set #3

Construction
of the block:

Back
of
Quilt

Ted's Quilt
By Kathryn Small, Westwood, CA

T Quilt
By
Mary
Ellen
Hopkins

Four blocks for sets 3 and 4:

1   2   3   4

Set #4
My Favorite

1   3

2   4

Repeat

Set #5
Tumbling T's

1   3

2   4

Repeat

Little Ribbon Bow

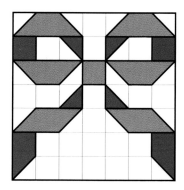

When you float this block, if blocks are made by several people, they can now be trimmed to identical size.

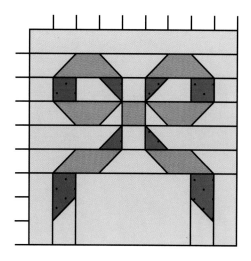

Block #229 from "It's Okay..." book. This block is made the old fashioned way using PPT'S.

First game plan-redrafted using the Connector technique and floating. First game plan breaks down to a 9-Patch, sewn together in horizontal rows.

Second game plan breakdown.

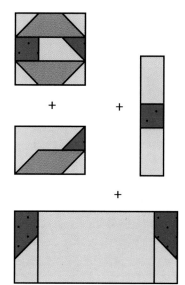

Little Ribbon Bow
By Barbara Spielberg, West Los Angeles, CA

Sailboats

This is a keep a "lookout" pattern that can be sewn using the new Connector technique.

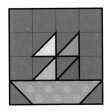

traditional pattern

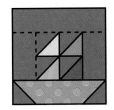

adapted pattern using new Connector technique

1      Make these first - can either be perfect pieced triangles or printed triangles like I used in the quilt pictured below.

2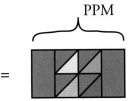

PPM

3   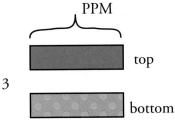   top

bottom

4

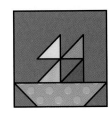

5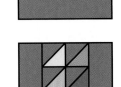

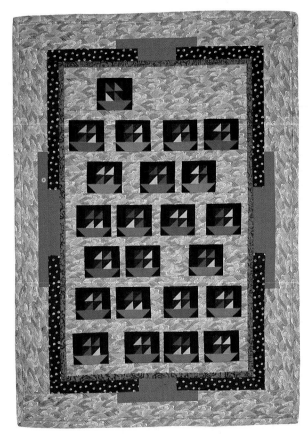

Quilt Back

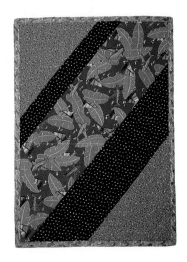

Sailboats
By Mary Ellen Hopkins

... and now
for something
a little ...

different

g
n
i
s h a r n e r
o
c

What is Sharing the Corner?
It is a different approach
to piecing blocks to give a
design a new look. You will see
which blocks can share a corner,
how to do it, and the dramatically
different look that Sharing the
Corner can give these blocks.

When can I Share the Corner?

When the opposite corners of a block are exactly the same and all four corners are the same size

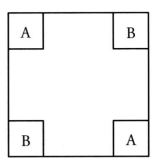

How do I Share the Corner?

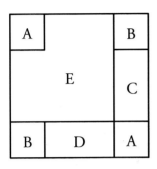

1. First look at the block as having parts A, B, C, D, and E as shown.

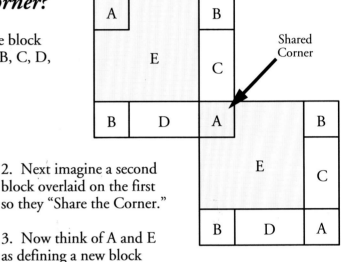

Shared Corner

2. Next imagine a second block overlaid on the first so they "Share the Corner."

3. Now think of A and E as defining a new block (yellow shaded area.)

4. Then imagine another of your original blocks sharing the opposite corner. This creates a second block (shaded grey) made from the remainder of the original block (areas B, C, and D) and an additional area of "background" (F).

5. Finally, construct the two new blocks and alternate to get the shared corner design. The construction of these blocks may vary depending on the design — see the Roman Cross layout later in this section.

Sharing The Corner With...

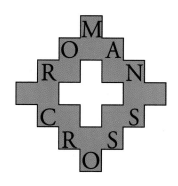

Let's start with the Roman Cross from "It's Okay...", page 92.

Now, redraft it in a straight rectangle.

You see it meets the requirements for sharing the corner, so...

Redraft it to share the corner. There are now two blocks, (each made from smaller pieced blocks) as indicated by solid lines. The piecing is shown on the following page.

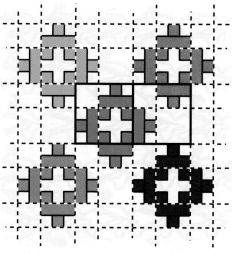

You might want to make one of these for each group you belong to (pinochle, guild, polo team...) and have members sign the blocks.

Straight Set Roman Cross
(without sharing the corner)
By
Mary Ellen Hopkins

Shared Corner Roman Cross
By
Mary Ellen Hopkins

Putting Roman Cross Together

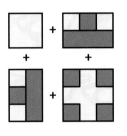 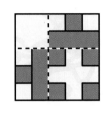

Step 1

Build the first block for each color Roman Cross using the pieced sections shown here.

Step 2

Lay out the pieced blocks together as shown on the right. Swap them around until you like the location of the blocks.

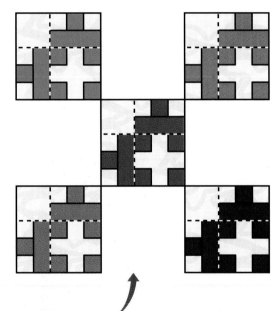

Step 3

Piece the alternate blocks as shown below. (Note that you can't do this until you are sure of the layout for the different colored blocks.)

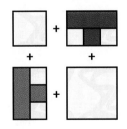 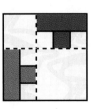

The quilt on the right of the preceding page was done using this method.

Now, let's take a look at what this design looks like on the diagonal as we examine the…

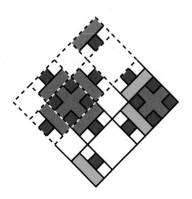

Poor Man's Scrap Album–Type Quilt

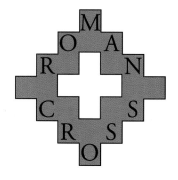

Poor Man's Scrap Album Quilt
By
Cheryl Trostud White
Calabasas, CA

Poor Man's Scrap Album Quilt
By
Mary Ellen Hopkins

This quilt is made of these pieces.

The above pieces make these blocks

Triangles
For Floating

Triangles
For Corners

Roman Cross
By Yachi Monarrez
Los Angeles, CA

Back of Quilt.

How Do Others Share The Corner?

Pinwheels

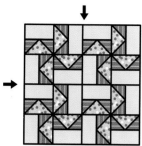

Traditional way of
piecing. 4 -Patch
marching in
perfect stiff rows.

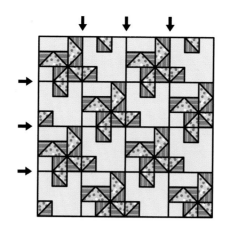

New way of piecing
with sharing a corner.

2 -3 patch blocks
A and B

Milky Way

Traditional way of piecing.

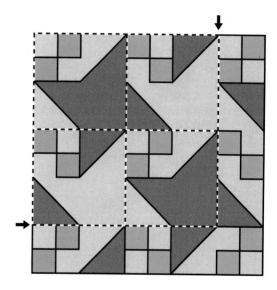

New way sharing the corner.

2 Blocks (A and B)
make up the repeat
shown above (see
page 79 in
"It's Okay…")

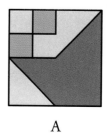

A   B

First Quilt For William
By
Mary Ellen Hopkins

Personal Private Showcase*

*Design your quilts on these pages and then add a photograph of your finished quilt.